Happiness is a good

Happiness is a good duck

by Matthew Martin

Originally published under the title 250 *Cartoons*

VINTAGE BOOKS • A DIVISION OF RANDOM HOUSE • NEW YORK

First Vintage Books Edition, December 1988

LIBRARY OF CONGRESS CATALOGING-IN-PUBLICATION DATA
Martin, Matthew, 1952–
Happiness is a good duck.
Originally published 1986 under title: 250 cartoons.
1. Australian wit and humor, Pictorial.   I. Title.
NC1759.M37A4   1988   741.5′994   88-40047
ISBN 0-394-75959-1 (pbk.)

Author photo by Rachel Knepfer

Manufactured in the United States of America

10 9 8 7 6 5 4 3 2 1

To David Dale
My second most
severe critic
With gratitude

How to shave

1 IMPORTANT: Practise with balloon first.

2 Then shave face

3 More practice needed. m.

Unlikely accidents...

Slipping on a banana skin

Cleaning a gun when it goes off

Grazing your knees

The problems of being a werewolf

Harold I'm a werewolf.

You're not kidding

I howl at the full moon

Tsk.

I eat small children. I need help!

Sorry Alice, I can't bear children. Ha ha ha

4

How to kill a bee...

First let it sting you.

Then it dies.

Then hit it with an axe.

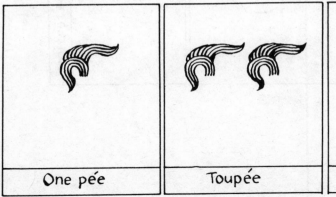

One pée

Toupée

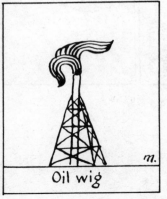

Oil wig

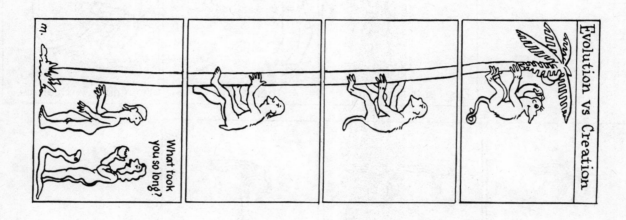

Leech-o-nine-tails
(Suckers for punishment)

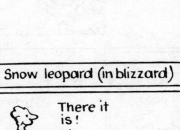

Snow leopard (in blizzard)

There it is!

Spotted leopard

8

9

A shooting accident

CLICK!

I'm sorry. I thought it was loaded.

m.

Operating Theatre

You are going to sleep.

Yawn

m.

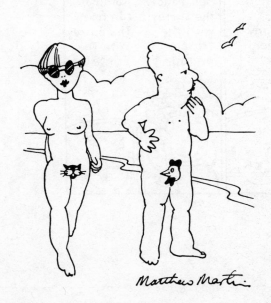

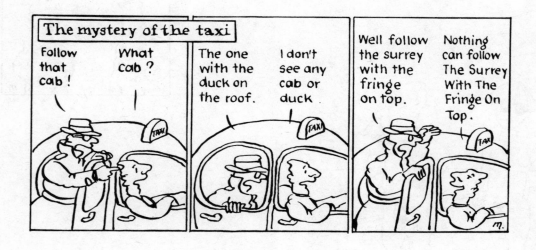

14

15

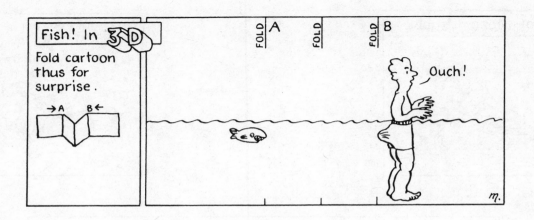

17

Living Sculpture

AAGH!

You've seen one christening you've seen them all. Let's play golf.

Yeah.   Fine.

The Aberration of the Magi

RESERVED

EXTROVERTED

Waiter there's a rat in my soup.

It is rat soup sir.

Oh. I feel such a fool.

It happens all the time.

Um... I didn't order rat soup.

Yes, that happens all the time, too.

On a Peking street

Fang finds relief...

...incurs citizens' wrath...

...and sees the aura of his wees.

21

27

Music listing

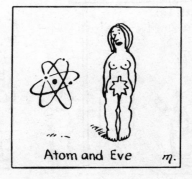

32

29

37

German Bank joke

I vant to be a loan

m.

What *is* reality? A nice place to visit but I wouldn't want to live there

40

Sheep runs in nylon jacket...

.. builds up static electricity ...

.. and charges battery.

LOOK OUT! HE'S GOT A GUN!

Adam and Edam

43

45

46

48

The end of the
hunting season

Other animal innovations

Animal husbandry

Animal crackers in soup

Freud discovers animal magnetism

They both claim owner-ship of the cocky.

Simple. I shall cut it in half.

Ok Fine

Well Solomon, what now?

53

54

I went over Niagara Falls in a barrel.

I went over Niagara Falls with a fine-tooth comb.

I went around with Muhammad Ali but we don't speak any more.

Napoleon's over-coat

Napoleon's under-coat

San Francisco Bay

Do you know I'd like to bring you to orgasm?

No, but hum a few bars and I'll fake it.

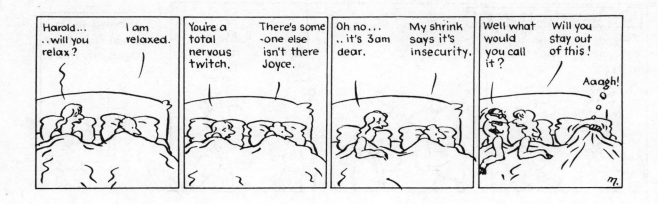

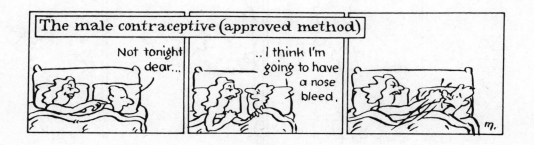

59

61

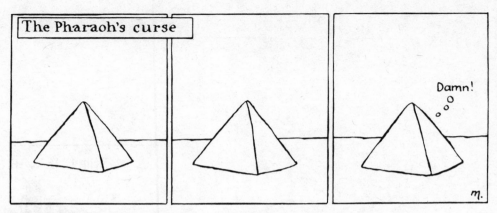

Petrified tree

Still Life with Censorshi█

66

Really Grand Opera

Is that a turkey on the camel?

No dear, that's the contralto.

Sounds like a turkey.

Wait. There is a turkey on the contralto.

Caruso never used a turkey.

Caruso wasn't a contralto.

At an epic play...

Have I missed much?

About three hours.

I had trouble parking the car.

We came in a cab.

Yes, I had trouble parking the cab.

Fine. Where's my husband?

Dr. Fee and team set out on the
Great G·spot Expedition of '82-'83

Down by the sea of porridge

We have determined that rats would be the dominant species after a nuclear war.

Tuesday	Monday	Tuesday again

Tuesday

How does yesterday look?

Exciting.

Monday

Wow this is fun.

Tomorrow looks boring

Tuesday again

Still, we have our memories.

My head's stuck!

Great Pigeon Monument
(Proposal rejected) m.

See?
Simple.
Now you
try.

Thanks.

Beauty and the Beast

I truly
love you
Mr Beast.

Oh!
Happiness
is mine.

Mr Beast!

It was
just a
mask.

Me
too.

Snap.

79

Sweet bird of youth

I am young
I am free
I live in a great
big tree

I am light
I am airy
I can fly just like
a fairy

I get drunk
I fall over
I go home with
my friend Rover

87

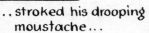

93

Not thinking of José			
"No way, Julio!"	Nope... "No way, Rodrigez!"	Nah...	Looks like it's "Au contraire!" again.

Irreconcilable Differences
Peace offering   Peace off

A streaker named Desire

How to drown yourself

1. Practise with a bucket of water.

2. Remove head from buc...

3. Ignore step 2.

How to make a zombie

1. Kill your victim

2. Bring victim back to life

3. Have victim ride train to work.

95

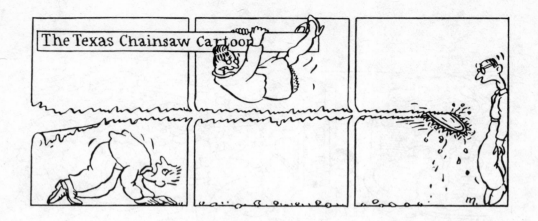

The Texas Chainsaw Cartoon

How to make a forgery

1. Study original closely

2. Make copy

3. Ask friends to pick original

The John according to
Saint Gospel

What did the Witch-doctor say at school?

You'll need an axe if you want to get a head.

Mr Reagan tries out his new hearing aid

Ok Mr President, we're testing now.

What did he say?

"Ok Mr President, we're testing now."

Good. I think you'll work out fine.

A pigeon's story...

What happened to you?

Well, I was just standing here...

..minding my own business...

...when that statue came over, squatted above me...

Ritual killing, AD2

Will you stop doing that!

Sorry hee hee

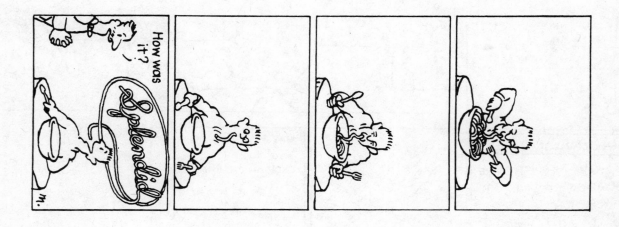

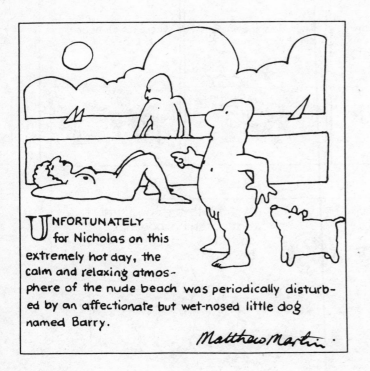

UNFORTUNATELY for Nicholas on this extremely hot day, the calm and relaxing atmosphere of the nude beach was periodically disturbed by an affectionate but wet-nosed little dog named Barry.

Matthew Martin.

Rescue robot

OK YOU'RE DOING FINE. NOW BRING YOUR LEFT FOOT DOWN...

m.

Life (revised edition)...

While you and I must struggle through

just keeping clean our noses

There is somewhere some lucky few

where it's all beer and roses

Well, that's a rhino, and that's a rhino poacher... ...so that... yes that *must* be the time .

The first assault on Troy...

Lady gives birth to baby on bench

The hard part was finding the wood.

A piano bar...

Do you know Hum A Few Bars And I'll Fake It?

Yes but I don't do requests.

The contraceptive bullet

Was that you I heard banging away last night?

He just put on his indicator then turned into a monster

110

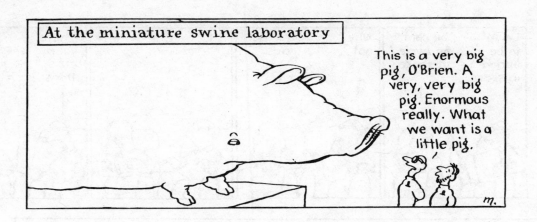

111

One Valentine's Day

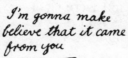

Noah's bus

Noah collected all the animals into the bus two by two.

Then he drove the bus to the top of the mountain.

But soon the windows were completey steamed over and the air became unbreathable.

Noah said, "I told you Lord, we need an ark."
"Ok, ok," said the Lord, "I was just testing you."

The elusive pig

Look!
Up there!
It's Halley's comet!

Hee
hee

118

119

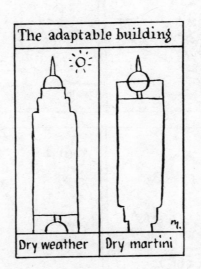

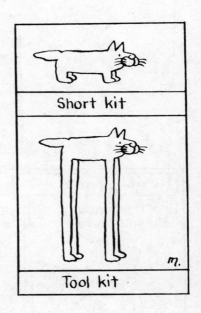

Breaking up a satanic circle

Matthew Martin was born in Broken Hill,
Australia, on April 1, 1952. Raised in a service
elevator and educated in spite of his schooling,
he is a lapsed atheist with no children. He
looks nothing like his cartoons.